How to make a
FRUIT SA

Deborah Chancellor

OXFORD
UNIVERSITY PRESS

Contents

Fruit salad

Fruit is good for you.

Fruit salad looks good and tastes good.

Find out how to make it.

Going shopping

First, you must go shopping.

Put some red apples in your basket.
Put in some satsumas.

Choosing the fruit

Choose some kiwi fruit and two or three bananas.
Check that the fruit is ripe.

Pick some pears and a bunch of green grapes.

Choose some strawberries.

Put all the fruit in your basket.

Paying for your shopping

Find some fruit juice.

You only need one carton.

Pay for your shopping at the till.
Then take it home.

Making the fruit salad

Ask an adult to help you make the fruit salad.

Peel the fruit and cut it into small pieces.
Be careful with the knife! Don't cut your fingers.

Ready to eat

Put all the fruit into a bowl.
Add some juice, then stir your fruit salad.

Now it is ready to eat!

13

Your fruit salad

grapes

satsuma

apple

What fruit will you put in your fruit salad?

banana

strawberry

pear

kiwi fruit

Index